100

Also by Alfred Brendel

Musical Thoughts and Afterthoughts

Music Sounded Out: Essays, Lectures, Interviews, Afterthoughts

ONE FINGER TOO MANY

ALFRED BRENDEL

ONE
FINGER
TOO
MANY

English versions by the author
with Richard Stokes

RANDOM HOUSE / NEW YORK

This work was originally published in Great Britain by Faber
and Faber Limited in 1998. "Three Tenors" and "Paradise"
originally appeared in *The New York Review of Books.*

In addition, the poems in this edition were originally published
in German in two volumes by Carl Hanser Verlag, Munich:
Fingerzeig (Copyright © 1996 by Carl Hanser Verlag München
Wien) and *Störendes Lachen Während Des Jaworts* (Copyright © 1997
by Carl Hanser Verlag München Wien).

Library of Congress Cataloging-in-Publication Data
Brendel, Alfred.
One finger too many / Alfred Brendel ; English versions
by the author with Richard Stokes.—1st ed.
p.   cm.
ISBN 0-375-50293-9 (acid-free paper)
I. Brendel, Alfred—Translations into English.
I. Stokes, Richard.   II. Title.
PT2662.R446O54   1999   831'.914—dc21   98-44869

website address: www.atrandom.com
Printed in the United States of America on acid-free paper
98765432
First U.S. Edition

Book design by J. K. Lambert

ONE FINGER TOO MANY

There was a pianist
who developed
a third index finger
not to play the piano with
though it sometimes did intervene
discreetly
in tricky passages
but to point things out
when both hands were busy

Once in a while
the finger shot from his nose
to expose an obstinate cougher in the hall
or emerged from beneath his tailcoat
beckoning a lady in the third row
In complicated fugues
you saw it rise to its full height
from under his shirt collar
indicating the theme in retrograde
Occasionally
when the harmony got muddled
it even turned against its owner
repeatedly knocking its knuckle
on his cranium

Whatever it wished to complain about
remained a mystery
for clearly the pianist was doing his best
and the audience
at such moments
held its breath
When subsequently
the finger disappeared

into the pianist's left upper pocket
one could sense
in the hall
a certain relief
The man with the videocamera
who had managed to record the scene
nodded off
and the critic
eager to remember the exact wording
wrote down the title of his piece
One finger too many

Quite an achievement
evening after evening
to pursue on stage
undaunted
without a trace of fatigue
if not with downright zeal
an activity
which most of us would rather keep private
namely
making love
both reviled and spurred on by the public
painstakingly supervised by the author
who
on top of it all
has entrusted the lovers with the burden of dialogue
a stunning coup de théâtre it has to be said
this discourse about the supernatural
delivered by the actors with calm assurance

Well-nigh incredible
how here
eight times a week
Saturday afternoons included
evidence is furnished
that
at the height of passion
reasoning of the appropriate clarity
can help you
blow your mind

When Godot finally arrived
it was a letdown
That he was limping
became evident from a distance
a small man with an outsize beard
over which
at times
he stumbled
cursing softly
Explaining himself
was not his style
Accounting for his deeds
did not suit him
So he'd rely on puns
something he was good at
Children thought him amusing
When he threw them sweets
they caught them in midair
like bears in a zoo
But no one ventured near him
for that
he was too unkempt
and his gaze
betrayed the evil eye
Had it not been for his luminous tail
he might yet have gone unrecognized
It kept moving through the village
long after its master
had vanished behind the hills

The monkey
who made himself useful
each Christmas
had almost become part of our family
Year after year
he'd arrive in a dinner jacket
put logs on the fire
decorate the Christmas tree
wait on us at meals
even manage to sing
Silent Night he sang with feeling
Only when laughing
was he prone to lose control
during moments of elation
he'd start to bleat
or cackle
until my mother raised an eyebrow
whereupon he quickly seized a bottle of champagne
and filled up the glasses
On Boxing Day
his keeper came as usual to collect him
Affectionately
we embraced each other
before
sporting hat and stick
he went to sit in the car
a good monkey
whom our mother urged us to ape

It could hardly have been worse
First the silver disappeared
Then the family portrait fell from the wall
Then it rained through the roof on Grandpa
Then Dorothy disgraced herself with the chauffeur
Then the piano teacher
stiff as a pole
was found beneath the concert grand
Then the car spluttered and stopped
The toy train was derailed
The chickens clucked their last
All the bulbs exploded
Someone started playing the trombone
That really was too much

When the actor began to study his part
he wondered
into which regions of himself
this would lead him
He found it full of contradictions
a character difficult to confine
to comedy
farce
mystery play
or melodrama
Of course one had to be versatile
change identity at will
wear a magician's hat
strut ceremoniously as a priest
fly through the air as a spirit
but also cut capers like a jester
pine as Pierrot
and play the cuckold
whose unintentional comedy
had to be expressed with discretion
or the wicked politician with the friendly face
a task
not overly ambitious yet gratifying
Only tragedy
he hoped
would bypass him
it aimed too high
featuring monuments not people
monuments disintegrating into rubble
when struck by fate
Better stick to the ridiculous
act helpless
a well-tried approach

Presenting heroes helpless
was the style of the day
In addition
one practiced a few heartfelt cries
just to be safe
In the end
one hardly knew where one belonged
not a bad state
come to think of it
keeping oneself open
and leaving it to the director
to tell you
who you were

After the big-game hunter
had delighted the crocodile
by falling into the river
the crocodile pondered
at which angle
the fleshy man
might best be consumed
feet-upward
head-downward
belly-inward
Or should one rather
to spare one's stomach
first savor the toes
before
bit by bit
picking one's way
toward the ears
Heartburn
should be countered
by sufficient salivation
his rifle deposited
for digestion's sake
on the riverbed

While the crocodile pursued these thoughts
the big-game hunter
with resolute strokes
had reached the riverbank
where
I'm sorry to say
he was eaten by a lion

What did she want
showing up like that
when he was half asleep
remarkably three-dimensional
scantily but expensively clad
Why didn't she leave him alone
exhausted as he was from mental exertion
why thrust herself upon him
pinch his cheek
alluring it had to be said
in spite or because of
her excessively large bosom
wrapping itself twice around him
an amorous octopus
cool as snakeskin
Perhaps she mistook him for Tarzan
whereas
used to crouching over his desk
he barely knew how to move his limbs
Perhaps she reveled in conquests
kept records
and gave marks
Perhaps she even loved him
that would be alarming
albeit flattering
One needed
in such circumstances
to decide
whether to free oneself from her clasp
a delicate undertaking
or face the fact

that in the end
eyes and mouth
would be covered by tentacles
and all consciousness
lovingly smothered

When Christo had wrapped the Three Tenors
on the balcony of La Scala
the civilized world fell unnaturally silent
Falsetto supplications
barely audible through the sackcloth
were registered
in horror and glee
by opera-lovers attending the spectacle
but where that desperate earsplitting top note
            issued from
remained uncertain
It may however be assumed
to have come from the middle
and more voluminous
of the celebrities
whose mummified contour
began to quiver
while
at his feet
an envoy from the world's freest country
voiced his concern about such curbing
if not gagging
of human communication
Opera buffs will be pleased to learn
that the wrapping
in gray plastic
of Robert Wilson and Peter Sellars
halfway up Cologne Cathedral
has been confirmed
and will commence
in due course

Leo
the one-eyed
is no Giant
And yet his only eye
as is the way with Giants
sits right in the middle of his forehead
When he cries
everything gushes from the same outlet
To compensate for this
he weeps twice as much
until a rivulet runs down his nose
and trickles onto his tie
Why does Leo cry
Does he chop onions
Is he emotional
Or does he shed tears of laughter
No he cries
because he would like
to do what we do
squint
leer
and above all
wink
at us twin-eyed
i.e. keeping one eye open
while the other
shut one
fraternizes

Anxiously
we all fall silent
when Theodore
in his old-fashioned white nightshirt
climbs the roof
arms outstretched
hands
clasping a large gray mouse
a stuffed toy it's believed
that propels him
like a mute irresistible motor

Whither
one wonders
does the mouse propel its Theodore
who steps out with perfect poise
lit by the moon
and trusts his mouse
his guardian
when he feels the need for protection

May the rodent-angel
pilot him back to safety
before the black cloud above
pulls the moon from under his feet
and darkness
lights his eyes

Keep calm at all costs

The still-warm corpse
lay at my feet
strangulation marks
under its doglike ears
Not a soul to be seen
How did the creature
get into the cloakroom
to hide behind my coat
The shock
when I saw him
hideously snorting
half man half beast
neither centaur nor harpy
scales feathers dreadlocks pinkish skin
a nose like an anteater
the first thing I got hold of
three legs evidently
two in front one supporting the rump
female legs with high-heeled shoes
a few other human features
mouth and eyes
malicious
but not without laughter lines
a thoroughly male mustache
the creature's sex uncertain
no time to discuss that now

I'd better run for it
before the other satyrs notice my absence
and raise the alarm

Now that all those composers from the hereafter
had begun to populate her house
there was not much left
to throw her off balance
She didn't bat an eyelid
when they inflicted music on her
endless Victorian oratorios
on her of all people
who
deaf in one ear
heard only half
what Mendelssohn or Bruch craved to communicate
It didn't matter to her
that Brahms
rested his beard on her shoulder
or Chopin
fed her poached eggs
And when Liszt
while dictating his latest choral works
stroked her hair electrifyingly
she did not demur
Mozart
however
blew her fuse
Inconsiderate as always
this ogre
joined her in the bathtub
and made her sing his obscene canons one after another
in duet
Thank heaven
the apparition vanished just in time
allowing at least one of the canons
to find its way onto paper

bristling with wrong notes of course
that served him right
since it was none of her fault
Quickly
she grabbed something to wear
bracing herself for the visit
of surly Rachmaninov

You're Woody Allen
said someone next to me
a woman with a crooked tooth

Not that I am aware of
I replied
and made myself a little smaller
My name is Attila the Hun

Nonsense
said the woman
coming closer and closer
You can't fool ME!

If you say so
I said
and felt myself shrink further

until I had shrunk so much
that she carried me away
me and my clarinet
inside her shopping bag

When Brahms
bit his own finger
it was Billroth
Professor Billroth
who told him sternly
Nice people
don't bite themselves Johannes
whereupon Brahms
stuck the bleeding finger
into his beard

Of course I love you
he said
you know that I love all women
Reason enough for the woman
to grab a knife
and stab
in the name of all women
the man with the capacious heart
and with him all men
to death

When the dadaist looked into the mirror
he saw some fetching contradictions
himself and his opposite
tomfoolery and method
sense within nonsense
anarchy and poise
a slice of the world
yet nothing at all
The mirror image showed
women children a sheep
Beethoven mustachioed
even little Jesus paid his respects
with his tongue stuck out of course
Not that any of this surprised him
he knew he was floating
as people in dreams float over flights of stairs
or keeping at least an airy balance
laughing with earnest eyes
muttering comical curses
gracefully howling
Might the contradictions vanish
if one persisted
long enough
in their midst

And once again
the Lord of the Universe
recorded a day of good works
three religious wars launched
several tornadoes let loose
a new brand of pestilence devised
utopias planted into souls
countless children successfully harmed
good reason
to grant oneself a moment's rest
do something lyrical
make this man gaze on that woman
light up her heart behind her breasts
mobilize
in her heartbeat
anguish and desire
fan a little hellfire

A sheep
addressed me as follows
True
you do not have my looks
my wool my curls
your voice
does not pierce the heart
your speech
fails to convey the essential
you do not run after rams
you love neither peace nor nature
sneeze in July
and disappear
at the slightest trickle of rain
beneath your umbrella

And yet
you remain one of us
Even black sheep do
Underneath your wolf's clothing
something frail and gentle
begs for protection
I salute you
little lamb at the shambles

Baaaah
I said

To compose
one reassuring line per day
to placate our public
with a positive gesture
this
we quite simply
owe ourselves
First of all

we breathe in deeply
and look into the mirror
until we like what we see
Then
we glance around the room
for a truly insignificant object
ignored by everyone
which we gaze at lovingly
a speck of dust maybe
that for us represents all galaxies
As soon as we feel the world to be good
or even wondrous
we hurry to our desk
hold our breath
and pen our panegyric

Whereupon
we breathe out
and leaf through the latest news from the Cosmos
grimly aware of the asteroid
which approaches
from somewhere out there
and will hit us
if by then
our own black hole
hasn't sucked us in

Before I visit the Bagels
nice acquaintances of mine
animal-lovers
I'm always ready for a drink
Gingerly
I step inside
There sits a dog
tail in the air
staring at me
I sidle past him into the lounge
where the next one's lurking
ready to run its bacteria-infested tongue
over my face
In the bathroom
resides a bitch
whose sour-smelling whelps
crawl all over my shoes
At coffee
a small but tough pug
jumps into my lap
In the garden
something huge aims itself at me
a St Bernard
and gleefully knocks me into the roses
As I take my leave
I'm bitten by Mr Bagel
Let's hope he doesn't have rabies
I say God bless
retreating backward
Right up to the crossroads
I hear him barking after me

When at dead of night the ghost appears
and starts prowling round the piano
then we know
Brahms has arrived
It wouldn't be quite so bad
if his cigar smell
didn't stink out the music room for days on end
Even worse though
is his piano-playing
This wading through chords and double octaves
wakes even the children from their deep sleep
Not Brahms again
they wail
and stop their ears
Out of tune and smoking
the piano stands there
when Brahms gets up
Brahms
he says several times
in a plaintive tenor
before leaving through the kitchen door

He sprang
from his mother's body
laughing
cheered on by the midwife
who caught him in midair
He rushed through classrooms and barracks
Laughing
swept through wars
Women loved him
as he somersaulted
laughing
into their laps
Laughing
he subjugated the country
his laughter
acquiring a sardonic note
When
unannounced
he stopped laughing for good
his subjects rebelled
Too many
had wanted to watch him die
laughing

The gentle Buddha
ensconced in his fat
dripping sometimes
in hot weather
numb with content

what happened
to make him jump up
howling in anger
hopping on one foot
before thudding to the floor
flailing his thousand redeeming arms
now irredeemably entangled
a raging knot
helplessly writhing on his back

Some knew what had happened
a snakebite in the foot
Others knew better
his bottom
had come to rest
on a bee
The fact was
he couldn't cope with peace any longer
It's a strain being holy
Now there he lies
and his disciples
horrified
wipe the foam from his mouth
disentangle his arms
and wait for his rage to blow over
the moon-face to smooth itself
the Divinity to sit there

in proper style
composed
silent
hands folded
eyes half-closed
imperturbable

When the old lady
first took the chicken to bed with her
she didn't give it a second thought

It was chilly outside
and the chicken
friendly by nature
slipped between the sheets

Actually
the old lady resembled a chicken
Like many chickens
she failed to finish sentences
shuffled her feet
and brooded

There was just one thing
the old lady couldn't foresee
The chicken next to her
was a sprightly chicken
cackled in its sleep
flew about the room when it dreamed
fluttered anxiously
while plucking out a few of its feathers
All of a sudden
it thudded onto the bed
climbed a pillow
and laid an egg

Having accomplished this task
it snored
as only chickens can
when they are pleased with themselves

At dawn
accommodating as she was
the old lady crowed
to make the chicken feel at home

Since Sunday
they can both be seen
pecking their corn among the poultry
jerkily moving their heads
or running away from the rooster
screaming

After arriving in paradise
we ask ourselves
skeptics to the last
what on earth is going on here
The deaf listen to music
while musicians have fallen silent
The dumb have acquired speech
while the eloquent start to babble
The lame run like weasels
when not darting through the air
We
the powerless
stay powerless
content
with but a tinge of regret
watching the ugly grow beautiful
angels with blackened wings
drop from the sky
and the serpent
aim at us
hissing from its tree

Holding in his hand
the invitation to play Othello
he felt a slight quiver
There must be a reason for it
he thought
After all there it was in black and white
Othello wouldn't have occurred to him
He was not the jealous type
Besides
he never raised his voice
mistrusted Moors
and hated Venice
On the other hand
how could one say no
That sort of chance didn't come twice
Helena Bonham-Carter as Desdemona
was naturally a big plus
and Malkovich as Iago
one could live with
It was now a question of showing one's mettle
finding a way to shout
roll one's eyes
hide one's BBC accent
develop a murderous passion
whisper distinctly
place the words VERY FORWARD indeed
Tomorrow
first thing
he'd start while the bath was running
and declaim like Demosthenes
though he didn't have a stammer
He'd lope around the kitchen table
because that's how Moors moved

and afterward
in front of the mirror
pull a black stocking over his face
just like a burglar
Would black burglars
use pink stockings
OK then a black stocking
with holes for the eyes
in which to highlight the whites
A blunt sword
would have to be found
and Helena's photo
stuck on the mirror
With the gentle creature
standing there before you
or kneeling
praying
could you bring yourself
noble as you are
to run her through
because of a handkerchief
with a blade
even if not for real
Of course people would be jealous
his colleagues at the office
not to mention
Hopkins and Branagh & Co
But he'd show them
There was no turning back
He would go mad
as no Olivier had e'er gone mad
and all the while so noble
that Hopkins would be sure

to clasp him as a brother in his arms
His fine nostrils would flare
as neither Branagh, nay, nor Malkovich
might ever counterfeit
Roses would he send to fair Helena
twice a day
the least one could do
for killing her incessantly
His better half would be amazed
when
at bedtime
he practiced on her
with a pillow

When asked
what he considered most important in life
Roderick answered
Opinions
To offer them
required no knowledge at all
a kind of sixth sense
enabled him
to express them spontaneously
and with conviction
At times
he'd hardly be aware
of what he was saying
something spoke through him
as if through a mouthpiece
dumbfounding experts
while dazzling the uninformed
Amazed
he'd hear himself pontificate
pull explanations from his hat
pronounce verdicts
intoxicated by self-confidence
overwhelmed by his own courage
until
when everyone had gone
he'd find himself sitting between half-empty bookshelves
dazed by the echo of his inner voice

During his recent recital
I saw my celebrated colleague Fischkemper
levitate above the piano
I could hardly believe my eyes
but there he hovered
while the piano keys
all by themselves
went on playing the E flat trill from opus 111
thus demonstrating
even to the staunchest skeptic
that a mystical experience
accessible to all
was being enacted

The poet of the keyboard
after treating himself to bread-and-honey
sat down
ten-thirty sharp
at his instrument
ready to mesmerize
an imaginary public
the music
the piano
and of course
himself

No one
ever dared open the windows
Fresh air
might harm the poetry
the music's aroma
to be savored undiluted
by ears flared like nostrils
craving nuances previously unfathomed

In actual fact
the music room smelt of cats
creatures he tolerated
provided they didn't sharpen their claws on his sofa
or deposit mice beneath the pedals
The poet of the piano
moved his fingers catlike
slunk and slithered
and mewed
when the music conveyed emotional hunger
Furtively
he would glance at the clock

a growl
by no means feline
had emerged from within
but twelve-thirty was nowhere near
and to quench his appetite for beauty
required all his attention

Thus
the pianist went on weaving his magic
movingly simple yet morbidly sophisticated
a rare combination
until the rattle of his alarm clock
interrupted him in the middle of a bar
Considering he'd played the Nocturne
almost seventeen times in a row
he felt entitled
to another bite of bread-and-honey

Wouldn't you
perhaps
like to become a hero
withstand tyrants
swallow fire in a circus
freeze coatless
in midwinter
conduct a hundred-piece orchestra
radiate from within
like Gérard Philipe
grab fate by the throat
à la Beethoven
persevere in matrimony
die gallantly
for a truth idea cause
not
however
before consigning as many as you can to their graves
stand erect
on a column
bid good-bye to this world
stately and stoical
as a martyr
let yourself be butchered
for your country

Be a man
We'll carry you on our shield
arrange for your posthumous fame

When angels come to visit
they love telling stories
tall ones especially
angels adore nonsense
inform us about God and the world
all made up
resemble young prophets
or birds of paradise
or beautiful winged women
flighty
yet always with that aura of noble innocence
even when they oppress you
smother you with their wings
open heaven
Mothers
perceive them as putti
to be cuddled
before they whirr away

Resting on monuments
they preen themselves like swallows

Actually
the life he led
with a wife
and seventeen stand-ins
wasn't so bad after all
It was telling them apart
that gave him trouble
Their noses though
noses and bosoms
rang a bell
and also
of course
their voices
since he was truly musical
But as they hardly spoke
he had them sing for him
That
sometimes
made him remember a name
The only one he'd recognize without fail
was the pretty stutterer
she stuttered so delightfully
When she didn't get past the first
s-s-syllable
he felt aroused
and drew the blinds

Next week he held auditions
Puccini and Lehár
something to look forward to
Accommodation and singing lessons
were free
Abdominal muscles and diaphragm

had always been his métier
Smoothness of line he inherited from Tauber
whereas technique
came more from Gigli
Young they had to be
When
in addition
they showed talent
talent and devotion
he could be relied upon
and the palace kitchen was renowned

The mouse felt
that beyond the world of mice
another
higher
deeper
inner
reality
transcended
all gnawing
squeaking
nibbling
ways of the world
like one colossal cheese
awesome
yellowish
with lovely holes
irrefutably sublime

One could stand there
left foot slightly forward
concentrated yet relaxed
a mature man
neither arrogant nor subservient
and wait for the audience to be silent
silent and attentive
before one started to laugh
explosively
to the point where somebody joined in
or
in a serious country like Italy
shook his head

One could then
aim a fire hose at the first row
unless one preferred to bow politely
sit down
and play something by Brom Brehm Brums
sorry Brahms
while releasing simultaneously a handful of mice
in order to make the ladies climb onto their chairs
squeak in terror
and pull their skirts over their heads
a maneuver
that unfailingly makes the mice
take flight

One could leave the hall via the fire escape
equipped with beard and cigar

to sign autographs at the nearby coffeehouse
Sincerely Brahms
on napkins and handkerchiefs
blouses and bosoms
on earlobes just Brms

Looking at his watch
his face fell
Where on earth was Josephine
In five minutes
he knew the world would end
an event
he'd rather not witness alone
Clearly
she'd be standing in front of the mirror
putting on eyeliner
stepping out of one shoe into another
or rummaging through her jewelry
The sky had acquired a greenish tint
tiny puffs of smoke appeared
while
under his feet
there was a suspicious crackle
A bang
not unduly loud
reached his ear
before he fainted
When he awoke
someone was sprinkling him with water
The world was still there
Josephine
wearing an enormous hat
opened the terrace door
and said
Was that it

In the ongoing feud
between the bearded and the beardless
the bearded
strive to fasten beards on the beardless
whereas the beardless
with the help of enormous scissors
do their utmost
to remove the bearded's beards
Exposing the face
nauseates the bearded
concealing it
offends the beardless beyond measure
The beard
according to the bearded
has forever served
to veil areas of nudity
among which the face undoubtedly figures
Decency demands
that the faces of our fellow citizens
be concealed behind beards
Bunkum
cry the beardless
It is by baring the face
that the world is freed from deceit and deception
Beardless
the face speaks for itself
an altar of sincerity
to which our hearts go out
In recent skirmishes
positions seem to have hardened
One hears of horsehair
glued on the beardless
while the foe

replying in kind
rids the bearded of their beards
by ripping them out
Events
are being closely monitored
by barbers and hairdressers

The Coughers of Cologne
have joined forces with the Cologne Clappers
and established the Cough and Clap Society
a non-profit-making organization
whose aim it is
to guarantee each concertgoer's right
to cough and applaud
Attempts by unfeeling artists or impresarios
to question such privileges
have led to a Coughers and Clappers initiative
Members are required to applaud
immediately after sublime codas
and cough distinctly
during expressive silences
Distinct coughing is of paramount importance
to stifle or muffle it
forbidden on pain of expulsion
Coughers of outstanding tenacity
are awarded the Coughing Rhinemaiden
a handsome if slightly baroque appendage
to be worn around the neck
The C & C's recent merger
with the New York Sneezers
and the London Whistlers
raises high hopes
for Cologne's musical future

Should one laugh
laugh or giggle
at what
on what occasion
During funerals
would be obviously wrong
and tasteless
during sermons trials acts of parliament
not even a smile
during sex
that's hardly feasible
either you make love
or you laugh

When something IS funny
by all means laugh
by all means laugh

but the way you laugh
the know-how
is essential
all-important
a whole repertoire
must be developed
from snigger to roar
the tone
occasionally spiteful
yet always hearty

Considerate
it should always be
neither shrill nor snorting
embarrassed
always goes down well

Laughing your way
out of blunders
is always disarming

The right dose though
is crucial
from a terse huh
to tears peals scales
Be sure however
not to laugh yourself silly
you might end up
a laughingstock

Responsible nails
demand to be hit on the head
anvils of bluntness
martyrs of the accurately aimed blow
heroes in the service of boldness and brevity
hardened flatheads though
whose malicious glee knows no bounds
when
missing his target
the daredevil aphorist
manages to flatten his thumb

When Mozart was murdered
no one
not even Haydn
would have guessed
that it was Beethoven
who had committed the wicked deed
During an outing
while Mozart
exhausted from playing leapfrog
was resting in the grass
Beethoven
disguised as Salieri
approached
slinking like a tomcat
and trickled poison
into Mozart's matchless ear

At this point
it should be mentioned
that there was
in Beethoven's life
a closely guarded secret
Beethoven was BLACK
and Mozart had FOUND OUT
After one of Beethoven's wondrous improvisations
Mozart
had whispered to Süssmayr
Not bad for a nigger
Now there he lay
with poison racing through his veins

Laughing grimly
the culprit sneaked away
in full possession of the key of C minor
which
from now on
would be his

To walk through people stone-faced
reaps its own rewards
After a short while
one feels like a monument
removed from reality
No twitching around the mouth
no grin
no wink
nor mocking frown
disfigures our weatherproof countenance
No smile of recognition
heartens the passer-by with the outstretched hand
Like waiters in a restaurant
we look past or through him
until he withdraws his hand
and hastens to greet someone else
At home
we dance grimacing across the floor
before our facial muscles
give in to fatigue

Who will provide us with the missing
final
fourth or seventh Act
in which Tristan and Isolde
skeptics at last
enter into a marriage of convenience
Lulu is resurrected as Vestal Virgin
and Sarastro hands over his three sacerdotal chords
to the Queen of Night

Who will offer us the Act to end all Acts
in which Norma
with laryngitis looming
graces the stage as a mute apparition
Don Giovanni
atones for his sins among Christmas angels in heaven
and Florestan
the cruel usurper
throws Leonore into the dungeon

Who will bestow on us the longed-for
the ultimate finale
that renders perfection more perfect
restores disorder
puts toy trumpets in the mouths of Valhalla's Gods
and transforms Constanze into a hen
who
clucking ferociously
makes off behind the Seraglio

No
is hard to refute
It defies the impudent gods
draws boundaries
resolutely rational

When it puffs itself up
becomes coquettish
clamours for rebellion
we shall not submit to its lure
Let one No resist the other
the precise resist the imprecise

Let us use our Yes
sparingly
friendly but hesitant
Once it overwhelms us
it wipes us out

Those little men
who wander silently through rooms by night
and create confusion
they only visit orderly people
the more orderly the better
Books are a favorite target
They can turn them back to front
or upside down
All French literature
suddenly surfaces in the laundry closet
while the laundry ends up
oddly enough
in the larder next to the preserves
Hardworking creatures they are
capable of Herculean deeds
Recently
they dragged
no one knows how
the grand piano into the nursery
and stuffed it with soft toys
a banquet for the field mice
who love to camp in pianos at Christmas
Once the little men have settled in
you won't get rid of them
unless the little women intervene
They brandish their brooms
and chase the little men away
That's what they're like these days
little women

When FUFLUNS
the God of Rapture
looked on Hildegarde
a comely woman
goose pimples instantly tingled up her arms
crept like an army of ants
over shoulders and neck
reached the crown of her head
and made her hair bristle
like a hedgehog a wire brush or a broom
if not a witch or Medusa
A loud purring
like that of cats sewing machines or hydraulic pumps
emerged from her throat
punctuated by sighs of pleasure
and an occasional cry of FLUNSY
Eyes rolled toward heaven
Hildegarde resembled a seicento martyr
while her body's elliptical undulations
recalled those of Indian temple dancers
or writhing snakes shedding their skins
At that moment
FLAUSIA
the Goddess of Thrift Reason and Undernourishment
called FUFLUNS to order
whereupon
being her husband
he withdrew in confusion
Ever since
Hildegarde has been prone
to intermittent moments of stupor
mouthing FLUNSY
with lips like a trumpet

We are the rooster and the hen
We're also little chickens
And what about the egg
Who is the egg
WE ARE THE EGG
the yolk as well as the white
Furthermore
we are the fox
that gobbles the hens

Gosh we're everything

The news that
in the Tritsch-Tratsch Polka
a very cheerful piece of music
the Holy Ghost lay lurking
was not
for some of us
entirely unexpected
Confirmation of our suspicions
was supplied by a certain Alois
whose razor-sharp ear
detected in the Waltz King's opus 214
the unmistakable voice of God
Spurred on by Alois
we have since found ourselves
in brisk two-four polka tempo
heading straight for the Almighty
blissfully traversing his eighteen
or was it thirty-three
celestial spheres
which now
one after the other
open up before us
granting entry to all those
dancing in Alois's wake
encouraged now and again by a clip on the ear
a source of spiritual inspiration to be sure
while still keeping strictly
or stritschly in step
left right
Nothing must disturb the sense of harmony
Since both proffered cheeks
glow so radiantly
why not present one's back as well

on which Alois
tritsch tratsch
might crack his whip

The moment has arrived
to write a love poem   .
Most of you
will be familiar with the feeling
But finding the words
the candid tone
the faint tremor of the voice
this is what we'll try to accomplish today
To explain anything
would be a mistake
faced with countless ambiguities
our readers would desert us in droves
Rather
we should determine
whom or what we propose to love
women children dogs mankind the universe
I personally would disregard dogs
and target the brunette next door
With a bit of luck
she'll turn into another Laura
or Suleika
Those keen on detail
should concentrate on a particular feature
the chin the back of the knee the curve of a bosom
Others
by contrast
are bound to use a broader canvas
command a legion of Lauras
embrace one or all of the gods
As for style and technique
paradox euphemism or aposiopesis
would suit our purpose
Now kindly start writing

Waking
I found myself on my back

> *Surely not*
> *When*
> *let me ask you*
> *did a camel*
> *ever adopt a supine position*

You've guessed it
the humps had gone

Standing up
I turned my head
Nothing undulated there
only my self-possession wavered
Where
without bulges
did one belong
Did one still pass for a camel
or had one degenerated into a horse
No chance now of a job in *Aida*
unless they fastened rucksacks to my back
Maybe I could hire myself out as a steed
resaddle for *The Valkyrie*
a fat woman astride me
If nothing else worked out
there was always the needle's eye
a demanding act
for which one had to fast forever
get thinner and flatter
and twirl the left foot for threading

ACKNOWLEDGMENTS

The author wishes to thank Michael Morley and Susan Hohl for their work on some of these texts. The version of "Brahms II" is almost entirely Michael Morley's, who also contributed passages to "Othello" and "Tritsch-Tratsch." "Buddha" and "Sultan" are based on Susan Hohl's translations, and some of her suggestions elsewhere have been gratefully incorporated. For their encouragement and critical advice, I am greatly indebted to Andrew Motion and A. Alvarez. Above all, my thanks go to Richard Stokes, without whom this book would not have been possible.

There are, among my muses, a number of old ladies. One of them stopped in front of the bench I was sitting on at New York's Museum of Modern Art, pointed at me, and said, "Are you Woody Allen?"

Another one belonged to a group that regularly listens to Johann Strauss's "Tritsch-Tratsch Polka" in order to get in touch with the Holy Ghost. As she explained on television, her aim was to enter the "eighteen, no pardon me, the thirty-three" circles of Heaven. Everything else in the poem, including Alois, sprang from my depraved imagination.

Fufluns is the name of an Etruscan god, akin to Dionysos; Johannes Brahms that of a Vienna-based composer, whose D minor Concerto has given me boundless pleasure.

A. B.

CONTENTS

ABOUT THE AUTHOR

ALFRED BRENDEL was born in 1931 in Wiesenberg, Moravia. Though largely self-taught after his sixteenth year, he attended master classes by pianists Edwin Fischer (Lucerne) and Eduard Steuermann (Salzburg). He moved first to Vienna and later to London, and became one of this century's most widely respected pianists and classical recording artists, performing on the major concert stages of the world. Mr. Brendel has elicited unusual praise from some of the most distinguished individuals of our time. "He studies the composers, he understands them, he enters their skins," wrote the late Sir Isaiah Berlin. Among the numerous awards Mr. Brendel has received are honorary doctorates from the universities of London, Oxford, and Yale.

A writer as well as a musician, Mr. Brendel has published two collections of musical essays, *Musical Thoughts and Afterthoughts* and *Music Sounded Out*. Entering a new phase of his iconoclastic career, this legendary pianist now turns to verse. *One Finger Too Many* is his first book of poetry in English.

ABOUT THE TYPE

This book was set in Centaur, a typeface designed by the American typographer Bruce Rogers in 1929. Centaur was a typeface that Rogers adapted from the fifteenth-century type of Nicholas Jenson and modified in 1948 for a cutting by the Monotype Corporation.